Business Analysis Methodology Book

* Including a real life project case study

ISBN: 978-605-86037-3-8

About the Author

Emrah Yayıcı contributes to IIBA® (International Institute of Business Analysis) as a chapter President. He is the author of the best-selling *Business Analyst's Mentor Book* and *UX Design and Usability Mentor Book.*

He is one of the managing partners of UXservices, BA-Works and Keytorc. He started his career as a technology and management consultant at Arthur Andersen and Accenture. Afterward he led global enterprise transformation projects at Beko-Grundig Electronics.

During his career he has managed multinational and cross-functional project teams in banking, insurance, telecommunications, media, consumer electronics, IT industries, and startups.

He also contributed to UXPA (User Experience Professionals Association) as a member and ISTQB® (International Software Testing Board) as a former international board member.

He is now sharing his experience about business analysis, business development, entrepreneurship, product development, customer experience design, UX design, usability, and quality assurance by publishing articles and books, leading training sessions, and speaking at conferences.

Preface

Project teams usually have tight deadlines and limited budgets to develop and release new

- Software,

- Technological products,

- Mobile applications,

- E-businesses,

- Business solutions and,

- Business processes.

C-suite executives, investors and business unit managers always want to get quick and innovative results and rarely accept putting the brakes on the launch.

This book explains how high-performing companies overcome this challenge by using business analysis tools and techniques such as:

- User stories

- Use cases

- MVP (minimum viable product)

- Requirements documents

- User interface prototypes

- Lean UX (user experience) design

- Vision and scope documents

- Business cases

- Feasibility analysis

- Personas and user profiles

- Product backlogs

- Usability tests

and by applying lean principles.

A real life case study with sample project documents and diagrams is used to more practically explain these international tools, techniques, and lean principles to a broad range of practitioners, including:

- Business analysts, systems analysts, developers, and project managers

- Entrepreneurs, consultants, product managers, and product owners

- UX designers and marketing specialists.

C-suite executives and managers can also use this book as a quick and effective guide to:

- Foster innovation,

- Reduce time to market,

- Prevent waste, and

- Maximize project return on investment at their companies.

Table of Contents

1. Lean Principles to Achieve Innovation, Quality and Project Speed

High-performance companies achieve innovation, speed and quality by injecting the following lean principles into their DNA:

1. Be Value Oriented

- At each project, focus on generating *outcomes* (value) rather than *outputs* (deliverables).

- Always prioritize product features; focus on "must-have" rather than "nice-to-have" ones.

- Eliminate the waste of low-priority features that are not essential for customers.

2. Be Customer Centered

- Be like the sun but not the moon; illuminate yourself with the light of your own customers instead of your competitors.

  Concentrate on being more responsive to the needs of your target customers instead of benchmarking yourself with your competitors.

- Be *customer centric* rather than *product centric*. Consider products not as an objective but as a tool to meet your customers' needs.

- Develop products around your customers. Always listen closely to the "voice of your customers". Set up and maintain a continuous customer feedback loop.

- Ask customers about their needs but not their proposed solutions.

  Remember Henry Ford's famous quotation: "If I had asked people what they wanted, they would have said faster horses."

3. Be Iterative

- Think big, but start small.

- Be patient; remember that Rome was not built in a day.

- Move evolutionary rather than revolutionary:

    o   Use prototypes to gather early customer feedback.

    o   At the initial iteration, release a core version of the product including only high-priority features.

    o   In following iterations, use customer feedback from previous releases to refine the product by adding, updating, and even dropping features.

    o   Iterate until the product satisfies business and customer needs.

4. Be Simplistic

- Remember that less is *much* more. Do not complicate it.

- Focus on "just enough" and what is really necessary to satisfy customer needs.

- Appreciate downsizing the product by removing nonessential features, rather than upsizing it with bells and whistles.

- In determining product features, think as if you are decorating a small house. Don't make your users feel claustrophobic as if they're in a small, crowded space with a lot of furniture.

5. Don't Be Afraid of Early Failure

- Remember the famous quotation from American scientist and author Dr. James Jay Horning: "Good judgment comes from experience. Experience comes from bad judgment."

- Be adaptive, learn early from failures in initial iterations, and use this experience for later ones.

- Focus on *kaizen*, which means continuous improvement, by using lessons learned at previous iterations.

6. Optimize the Work Flow

- Act "just in time". Requirements analysis and design artifacts represent WIP (work in process) inventories in development lifecycle.

  Create them at the right time and with sufficient detail to prevent *WIP-level waste.*

2. Project Portfolio and Demand Management

To get maximum return on investment (ROI), every single project in a company should support corporate strategies. In other words, each project's objectives (business requirements) should be aligned with corporate strategies. Otherwise company resources are rooted in the wrong direction, and that results in *project portfolio-level waste.*

To ensure strategic alignment and prevent waste, requests from all business units within the company for new and enhanced software and technological products should be received, evaluated, and prioritized by a dedicated group of people.

In large-scale companies, this dedicated group may be a separate enterprise architecture team that works in coordination with company executives to understand business strategies, evaluate business unit requests against these strategies and steer technical teams in building products that meet today's and tomorrow's business and customer needs.

Since development of software and technological products takes a considerable amount of time, enterprise architects should guide technical teams in creating a flexible technical architecture that can serve both today's and tomorrow's new product development initiatives. Otherwise technical limitations become a bottleneck rather than an enabler for the company.

The enterprise architecture profession requires business knowledge, technical skills, and the ability to see the big picture with a bird's-eye view. Hence the most suitable people to fill enterprise architecture positions are experienced business analysts, product managers, and project managers who gain these competencies naturally as part of their profession. Thus in small- and midsized companies, project management offices (PMOs), product management teams, or a team of experienced business analysts should be responsible for evaluating and prioritizing product development/enhancement requests from all business units and ensuring the alignment of business and technical architectures.

Air Traffic Control Tower

In our clients, we witness an overwhelming number of new or enhanced software and technological product development requests from business units. Managing these requests is like managing the air traffic control tower at a very busy airport.

A huge number of requests waiting in the demand management pipeline creates a high *technical debt.*

Despite all their hard work, most technical departments are blamed for not being able to meet the expectations of business units. Business units mostly criticize technical departments for not delivering new or enhanced products fast enough.

According to Einstein's relativity theory, observations that you make about time differ from observations of others who are moving at different speeds. Similarly, project durations are relative for technical teams and business units of the same company. While six months will be considered a challenging time frame by most technical teams to develop a new product, it will be considered as a long duration by business units.

If delivered late, product development projects lose their importance for the business due to rapidly changing market conditions and fierce time-to-market pressures.

If you search for the root cause of technical teams' latencies, you will see that they can only allocate limited time to the development of new products. They spend the majority of their time on an overwhelming number of enhancement/modification requests for existing products to "keep the lights on."

"Keep the Lights On" Projects

A high number of these enhancement/modification requests also demotivates business analysts, product managers, developers, and project managers because, instead of being involved in new and innovative projects, they have to spend their time firefighting existing products.

If the additional cost of these enhancement/modification requests are not tracked systematically, the total cost of ownership for existing products will reach a very high amount. Usually this total amount outweighs the replacement of the existing product with a new one and creates *product enhancement/modification-level waste.*

Sometimes enhancement/modification requests are classified under the same category with maintenance requests. This is also an inappropriate approach since maintenance is a different category, and its aim is to ensure continuous operation of a product rather than to enhance its attributes. Each product should have a separate maintenance and enhancement/modification track to identify the best time to totally replace it.

The status of these enhancement/modification requests should be continuously reviewed. Some of the requests waiting in the pipeline may become obsolete due to changing business conditions. These obsolete requests should be identified and eliminated to optimize the utilization of technical resources and prevent waste.

Case Study: Mobile Application Development Project

A local CEC (consumer electronics company) outsourced its requirements gathering, documentation, and analysis process to BA-Works.

Company Overview

The CEC sold TV sets, speakers, home cinema systems, and DVD players via independent dealer stores. These dealer stores were also responsible for product delivery and repair.

The CEC worked with an outsourced call center company that was only responsible for customer service. It had no direct sales to customers.

The CEC managed its procurement, inventory, accounting, and sales operations on an ERP system and marketing operations on a CRM system.

Business Need

The CEC's website was only being used to present product and campaign information. There were no sales on the web channel. At that time the CEC didn't have a mobile application.

For the last two years, discounted prices on e-commerce websites had been driving the CEC's customers to the competition.

To overcome this situation, the CMO (chief marketing officer) of the CEC was considering creating the company's own online sales channels. The CMO planned to initiate the online strategy with a mobile application. At that time other consumer electronics companies didn't have mobile applications for this local market. The CMO wanted to make the CEC the first consumer electronics company that used mobile as a sales channel. He discussed the mobile application idea with his team members and asked them to move forward.

The company's marketing business unit entered this request on the CEC's demand management system as an urgent, high-priority demand. They noted that they wanted to release a mobile sales channel earlier than competitors, and thus the project had to be completed within two months at the latest.

On the following pages, the lean approach, as applied to the development and release of the CEC's mobile application, is explained in detail to help readers better understand the relevant content in each chapter of the book.

3. Strategic Analysis and Scope Definition

The lean approach brings a purpose-led, value-oriented mindset that necessitates a shared vision among all project stakeholders.

Business analysts should start every project by defining the business requirements that explain the vision and value proposition of the product. Business requirements should clearly answer *why* customers need that specific product.

Business analysts should interview target customers at the beginning of the project and validate that the defined business requirements can resolve articulated customer needs.

Clear definition of business requirements at the beginning of the project steers every stakeholder in the same strategic direction. This mitigates the risk of scope creep due to potential change requests (CRs), which result in waste due to rework.

Depending on the size of the project, business requirements can be defined in different types of product scope documents:

1. Business-Case Document

In large-scale projects (usually called Type-A projects) that have enterprise-level impact, business requirements should be documented on a business-case document. The business-case document should include:

- Business requirements: to clarify why the new product is needed

- Scope: to define and prioritize product features that will satisfy specific goals and problems of target customers

- Context: to analyze which other products and systems the product will work in integration with

- Cost vs. benefit analysis: to better understand the feasibility of the new product. The feasibility of a new product should be analyzed based on the defined scope, because a feasible product may become infeasible depending on the selected features.

- Risks: to identify and mitigate possible negative consequences of releasing the new product.

2. Vision and Scope Document

For medium- and small-scale projects (usually called Type-B projects), business requirements should be documented on a vision and scope document. This document should include features of the proposed product that will be delivered in each release and provide context information that shows the high-level integration of the product with other products and systems.

3. SOW (Statement of Work) Document

For enhancement/modification requests (usually called Type-C projects) on existing products that usually last less than one month, there is no need for a business-case or vision and scope document. A clear explanation of the business need in a one-page SOW document is just enough to describe the scope of work. These requests are better fulfilled by a more agile approach without too much documentation.

Rippling Effect

On any scope document, business requirements should be defined in specific, purpose-led, achievable, and crystal clear statements.

A clear definition of business requirements at the start of the project is very important, because at later stages of the project, the functional, nonfunctional, and technical requirements, and the business rules of the product should be defined consistent with the business requirements. Wrong definition of business requirements will have an adverse rippling effect on all of these low-level requirements and business rules. This will result in waste due to a high number of CRs and defects.

Paradox of Choice

Having many features is not an indicator of elegance or quality in lean product development.

On the contrary, as psychologist Barry Schwartz describes it in his book *Paradox of Choice: Why More Is Less*, choice overload creates decision-making paralysis, anxiety, and stress rather than bringing more satisfaction to customers.

A lean approach, delivering "maximum value" with "just enough" features, is the ultimate goal. Having a formal prioritization process is one of the preconditions for applying this approach.

Without a prioritization process, business units feel free to request any product feature as if the project has unlimited resources. The features requested by business units should be prioritized according to two main criteria:

- business value and,

- implementation difficulty.

Business value depends on the alignment of a feature to business requirements and customer needs. The items with high business value and low implementation difficulty should be rated as high priority, while the ones with low business value and high implementation difficulty should be rated as low priority.

Business Value

High Priority (Must Have)	Medium Priority
Medium Priority	Low Priority (Nice to Have)

Implementation Difficulty

The rest of the features should be labeled as medium priority and prioritized according to their expected frequency of use. Medium priority features can be relabeled as high priority if they have high frequency of use. Otherwise, they move to the low priority quadrant.

Time to Market

When time to market is critical for the product, the project should be classified as a "fast-track" one. In these time-sensitive, fast-track projects, business analysts and managers should convince business units to focus on "must-have" features rather than "nice-to-have" features and try to generate "fair-value" outcomes in an iterative way.

80/20 Rule

Regardless of time-to-market constraints, business units are always eager to expand the scope of products by adding nice-to-have features. However, in our experience the majority of users only use a minority of the product features. This is big source of *scope-level waste*.

When business units insist on nice-to-have, low-priority features, business analysts and project managers should remind them of the famous phrase in Voltaire's poem "La Begueule": "perfect is the enemy of good." The phrase suggests that insisting on perfection often results in no improvement at all.

Benchmarking and Reverse Engineering

Business units also have a tendency to enlarge the product scope by benchmarking competitors' products and requesting all of their features.

Although benchmarking competitors' products is a fast way of determining product features, it is not appreciated at every phase of lean product development.

In a lean approach, project stakeholders should be looking at "what problems of my target customers should my product solve" instead of "what my competitors are doing."

After product features are defined, benchmarking can then be used to fasten later phases of product development by exploring how competitors implement similar features without reinventing the wheel.

It should also be remembered that even the best competitors don't always do the right things. Thus benchmarking can also result in copying competitors' mistakes. In one of BA-Works projects, our team was responsible for benchmarking the customer interaction channels of a global hotel chain with its competitors. During the study our team noticed that the majority of competitors had common right things and common wrong things on their customer-interaction channels (web, call center, mobile, and social media). This was a result of a copy-and-paste approach. Although copying competitors is a fast way, companies should first focus on finding ways to differentiate themselves in providing the best customer experience.

Core Version of a Product

The lean approach suggests the following flow in PDLC:

- Deploy the first release with a core version of the product, and get customer feedback as early as possible.

- At each following iteration, use previous customer feedback to refine the product by adding, updating, and even dropping features.

- Iterate until the product satisfies business requirements and customer needs.

The core version of a product should have a minimum set of features that can solve the main problem of target customers. Popular terms such as MVP (minimum viable product) and MMF (minimum marketable features) are used to define this core version of the product.

For instance, the core version of a golf car should at least have an engine, tires, steering wheel, brakes, seats, and a utility box. At the first release, even these limited core features may fulfill the basic customer need of transportation on a new golf field. The decision to add which nice-to-have features, such as cup holders, ice boxes, heated windshields, and sound systems, can be made later according to customer feedback on the core version of the car.

High-priority features on scope documents are the best candidates for the core version of the product. Medium- and low-priority features can be added to later releases according to customer feedback on the core version.

The priority of features may change based on customer feedback. A feature that was initially considered low-priority may later become a high-priority one. Similarly, a product feature that was initially considered a high-priority one may become obsolete if it doesn't deliver the desired value to customers.

For the CEC mobile application project, BA-Works' business analysts assessed the request from the marketing business unit. They marked this request as a Type-A project that had enterprise-level impact on sales channels. They were shocked when they saw that the marketing business unit planned to release the product only two months later.

Since it was a Type-A project, the analysts worked with the marketing business unit to prepare a business-case. The details of business-case document were as follows:

Business Requirements	Priority
Compete with e-commerce sites that sell consumer electronics products with discounted prices	High
Develop mobile channel earlier than other consumer electronics companies for first mover advantage	High
Benefit from instant buying requests of customers by fast and secure checkout with a few clicks on the mobile application	High
By mobile sales improve scale that is currently limited to the number and visibility of dealers	High
Implement an omnichannel strategy that improves dealer visibility, operations and sales	Medium
Position mobile application as a storefront where customers can view and compare products	Medium
Improve customer experience by always being connected with CEC customers, receiving their feedback and monitoring their digital footprints	Medium

Scope/Features	Priority	Business Requirement Mapping
Customers can view detailed information, such as images, prices, and technical specs of CEC products and buy them 24-7 by paying with their credit and debit cards	High	Compete with e-commerce sites that sell consumer electronics products with discounted prices Benefit from customers' instant buying requests with fast and secure checkout in just a few clicks on the mobile application By mobile sales improve scale that is currently limited to the number and visibility of dealers Position mobile application as a storefront where customers can

		view, compare and buy products
Customers can compare different models of CEC products	High	Position mobile application as a storefront where customers can view, compare and buy products
Customers can review and rate products	Medium	Improve customer experience by always being connected with CEC customers, receiving their feedback and monitoring their digital footprints
Customers can search which dealers have a specific product in stock	Medium	Implement an omnichannel strategy that improves dealer visibility and sales
Customers can track the status of their orders	Medium	Implement an omnichannel strategy that improves dealer visibility, operations, and sales
Customers can cancel orders	Medium	Implement an omnichannel strategy that improves dealer visibility, operations, and sales

Context

Our business analysts analyzed which existing systems such as:

- ERP (Enterprise Resource Planning),

- CRM (Customer Relationship Management),

- CMS (Content Management System),

- Dealer Management System

the mobile application needed to be integrated with to deliver the proposed features.

Cost vs. Benefit Analysis

Income from Mobile Channel	2012	2013	2014	2015	2016	2017
Sales Revenue without Mobile Channel		50,000,000	70,000,000	90,000,000	100,000,000	120,000,000
Sales Revenue with Mobile Channel		55,000,000	80,500,000	110,000,000	125,000,000	155,000,000
Sales Revenue from Mobile Channel		5,000,000	10,500,000	20,000,000	25,000,000	35,000,000
Net Profit Margin		5%				
Net Profit from Mobile Channel		250,000	525,000	1,000,000	1,250,000	1,750,000
Cost of Mobile Channel						
Initial Cost of Mobile Project	750,000					
Cost of Enhancement / Maintenance		150,000	100,000	50,000	50,000	50,000
Total Cost	750,000	150,000	100,000	50,000	50,000	50,000

Net Income From Mobile Project	(750,000)	100,000	425,000	950,000	1,200,000	1,700,000
Interest Rate	5%					
NPV	2,870,609					
Pay Back Year	2015					

According to the cost benefit analysis, the mobile application project had a positive NPV (net present value). It would payback in less than three years. This pay-back period was acceptable for the marketing business unit.

The project team also assessed the risks and defined the mitigation strategy.

Risks	Impact	Possibility	Priority	Mitigation
Sales on mobile channel may hurt the relationship with dealers which have been the sole seller of CEC	High	High	High	When a customer buys a product via mobile application, this order will be sent to the dealer

products until now. Dealers may react negatively to an alternative sales channel and become reluctant to sell CEC products.				at the nearest location to the customer. Dealer will deliver the product to the customer and will be paid a sales commission by CEC.
If the payment is not received on the mobile channel, instant buying desire of the customer may be lost while waiting for the dealer to contact him or her.	High	Medium	High	When a customer orders a product via mobile channel, he or she will have to make the payment in advance with a debit or credit card.
CEC may still not compete with other online channels due to their low prices	High	High	High	The prices on mobile channel should be discounted compared to regular prices. Dealers should be convinced that in total they will not lose income since orders via mobile channel will be redirected to them and their sales commission will compensate for the lost direct-sales income.
A customer searches for a dealer on the mobile application and then visits the store, but the product he or she is interested in is out of stock there.	Medium	Medium	Medium	There may be a feature on the mobile application that allows users to search which dealers have a specific product in stock and see the address of those stores.

4. Project Planning and Methodology Selection: Waterfall or Agile?

At the strategic level, successful enterprise architecture and demand management prevent *portfolio-level waste* by ensuring that company resources are utilized for the right product development projects that support company strategies.

To prevent *waste at tactical and operational levels*, resource utilization within the projects should be also optimized. This can be achieved by applying an appropriate methodology in every product development project.

Law of Entropy

As physics theory, everything in the universe has a bias to pass from a well-ordered state to a disordered state due to the law of entropy. This is also valid for product development projects. To prevent disorder and chaos, project teams should apply a methodology.

However, some managers fall into the trap of overstandardization and try to apply the same standard methodology to all of their projects. They even assign showy names such as Xagile, Waterscrum, and Scrumfall to these methodologies.

Since every project has different dynamics, it is better to apply a customized methodology that fits the specific project's needs instead of a one-size-fits-all approach. At a majority of companies, the most popular methodologies are waterfall and agile.

Waterfall or Agile?

According to the dialectical method in philosophy, "within themselves all things contain internal dialectical contradictions that are the primary cause of motion, change, and development in the world." Similarly, the internal contradictions and drawbacks of the waterfall methodology have been the driving force behind agile adoption.

The lean approach is usually associated with agile methodologies mainly due to its three manifesto statements:

1. "Working software over comprehensive documentation"

In scrum, a popular agile framework, requirements are defined as short and simple user stories (as a "role," I want "goal") on the product backlog by a business unit representative (the product owner). This minimizes the level of documentation and bureaucracy witnessed in waterfall projects.

2. "Customer collaboration over contract negotiation"

In agile projects the product owner and the development team work at the same location, which creates a more collaborative product development environment compared to waterfall projects.

3- "Responding to change over following a plan":

In waterfall projects, development waits for the completion of analysis and design phases. Thus, in a one-year project, it takes at least five to six months on average to get to the working parts of a product. This latency in delivery creates anxiety for business units who are impatient to see "quick" results. On the other hand, the agile team releases a working part of the product in a series of two to three weeklong "sprints" under the coordination of a "scrum master." The team velocity is adjusted iteratively by analyzing burn-down charts of previous sprints.

Agile projects' fast delivery of working products, starting from the first iteration, brings confidence to all stakeholders and enables the gathering of early customer feedback.

At dynamic business environments in which change is not the exception but the norm, applying agile methodology is more meaningful, because waterfall has low flexibility for changes on requirements. Any possible change to the requirements has an impact on the overall analysis and design artifacts. In agile environments a change to the requirements has no effect on the parts of the product that have not been analyzed or designed yet.

The product owner and the project team should conduct regular "grooming sessions" in agile projects. The aim of these sessions is to discuss customer feedback from previous sprints and update the product backlog by removing user stories that no longer have a value proposition. This also makes agile a more effective methodology in dynamic business environments.

However, applying agile methodology to every kind of project is not a correct strategy. It is still more appropriate to proceed with waterfall when:

- the product has intensive integration among its components;

- the colocation of project team members is not feasible;

- it is not possible for the team members to work only for a single project at a time; and

- there is high employee turnover, which runs the risk of losing project knowhow in case project team members leave the company.

Agile is iterative by nature. Although waterfall is a sequential methodology, it is still possible to make it more iterative by

- increasing the number of releases,

- benefiting from prototyping and review meetings to get early feedback from customers,

- minimizing the detail level of requirement documents by more effective usage of diagrams, and

- decomposing requirements into right granularity to improve understandability and traceability.

Quantum vs. Deterministic Models

Einstein's and Heisenberg's formulations are the most dominant models for explaining the laws of physics. Einstein did not believe in randomness (indeterminism), and he summarized this with his famous quotation, "As I have said so many times, God doesn't play dice with the world." On the other hand, Heisenberg's quantum model is based on the uncertainty principle, which is also called the "principle of indeterminacy."

Although these two theories are completely different, a physicist can still use both to make accurate calculations for different cases. While they mostly use Einstein's formulations to model atomic particles moving at velocities close to the speed of light, they use quantum formulations to model the behavior of subatomic particles.

We can associate waterfall methodology with Einstein's deterministic models and use it for projects that require big design upfront in relatively static business environments. On the other side, we can associate agile methodology with quantum theory's indeterminism due to its success in dynamic business environments with random business conditions.

Managers should not fall into an "either/or fallacy" by feeling they have to select either waterfall or agile. For some projects, including both static and dynamic conditions, even a hybrid strategy can be formulated that applies both waterfall and agile methodology for different phases within the same project. Waterfall can be applied at the initial phase of the project to release high-priority, core features of a product that has a complex architecture of many integrated components, and agile methodology can be applied in later phases to release remaining medium- and low-priority features.

For the CEC mobile application project, our team applied a similar hybrid methodology. Waterfall was applied at the first phase of the project, which lasted two months. At this phase only high-priority features were developed and released on a core version of the mobile application.

Feature	Priority	Business Requirement Mapping
Customers can view detailed information, such as images, prices, and technical specs of CEC products and buy them 24-7 by paying with their credit or debit cards.	High	Compete with e-commerce sites that sell consumer electronics products with discounted prices. Benefit from instant buying requests of customers by fast and secure checkout with a few clicks on the mobile application. By mobile sales improve scale that is currently limited to the number and visibility of dealers. Position mobile application as a storefront where customers can view, compare, and buy products.
Customers can compare different models of CEC products.	High	Position mobile application as a storefront where customers can view, compare, and buy products.

Feature	Priority	Part of Core Version?	Methodology	Phase
Customers can view detailed information, such as images, prices, and technical specs of CEC products and buy them 24-7 by paying with their credit or debit cards.	High	Yes	Waterfall	1
Customers can compare different models of CEC products.	High	Yes	Waterfall	1

The first phase of the project was delivered on time, within two months, and the following observations were made regarding the initial release of the product:

- A mobile sales channel was launched before competitors.

- The number of people who downloaded the CEC mobile application was more than expected.

- The number of customers who used the mobile application to view and order CEC products was more than projections on the business-case document.

This way, the CEC marketing business unit verified that the mobile application was a good idea. Even with a limited number of features, the product generated high value for CEC customers and satisfied business requirements.

Based on these initial results, the marketing business unit decided to initiate the second phase of the project to implement medium-priority features that were predefined on the business-case document.

Feature	Priority	Business Requirement Mapping
Customers can review and rate products	Medium	Improve customer experience by always being connected with CEC customers, receiving their feedback and monitoring their digital

		footprints.
Customers can search which dealers have a specific product in stock	Medium	Implement an omnichannel strategy that improves dealer visibility and sales.
Customers can track the status of their orders	Medium	Implement an omnichannel strategy that improves dealer visibility, operations, and sales.
Customers can cancel orders	Medium	Implement an omnichannel strategy that improves dealer visibility, operations, and sales.

In the second phase, the project team applied agile methodology. The project manager started to play the scrum master role. Since the CEC marketing team could not allocate a senior representative, the most experienced business analyst of the team played the role of product owner. The other business analysts became part of the agile team together with developers and software testers.

The medium-priority features of the mobile application were developed and released within two sprints, each of which lasted three weeks.

Feature	Priority	Part of Core Version?	Phase	Methodology	Sprint
Customers can review and rate products.	Medium	No	2	Agile	1
Customers can search which dealers have a specific product in stock.	Medium	No	2	Agile	1
Customers can track the status of their orders.	Medium	No	2	Agile	2
Customers can cancel orders.	Medium	No	2	Agile	2

After analyzing the customer feedback and mobile application usage logs of sprints one and two, the marketing business unit observed that:

- Customers definitely checked other customers' ratings and reviews before buying a product. This new feature was also very useful for listening to the voice of the customer, which was not possible to get from the dealer channel.

- Instead of contacting the call center, CEC customers were using the mobile application to track their orders. This resulted in extra savings, thanks to the reduction in outsourced call center costs.

CMO was happy to see that newly added features paid back very quickly. After analyzing usage logs and customer journey mapping studies, the marketing business unit decided to add some additional features to further increase the mobile application's utilization rate.

Feature	Priority	Business Requirement Mapping
Customers can rate and comment on dealer service quality after delivery and setup of the products.	Low	Implement an omnichannel strategy that improves dealer visibility, operations, and sales.
Customers are notified about campaigns and promotions when they are near to a CEC dealer.	Low	Recognize location of customers, and send them contextual offers to increase marketing return on investment.
Customers are rewarded with coupon codes when they connect to a CEC product via the CEC mobile application.	Low	Improve loyalty of customers.
Customers can login with social media accounts and share information about CEC products.	Low	Create evangelistic customers who share information about CEC products.

These new features were also implemented with agile methodology in two more sprints.

Feature	Priority	Part of Core Version?	Phase	Methodology	Sprint
Customers can rate and comment on dealer service quality after delivery and setup of the products.	Low	No	2	Agile	3
Customers are notified about campaigns and promotions when they are near to a CEC dealer.	Low	No	2	Agile	3
Customers are rewarded with coupon codes when they connect to a CEC product via mobile application.	Low	No	2	Agile	4
Customers can log in with social media accounts and share information about CEC products.	Low	No	2	Agile	4

After analyzing the customer feedback and mobile application usage logs of sprints three and four, the marketing business unit observed that:

- The product feature that sent coupon codes when customers connected to a CEC product via the CEC mobile application became very popular. Used by a high number of customers, it positively impacted cross-sell opportunities and customer loyalty.

- Customers were not as responsive as expected to the contextual offers sent via the mobile application. This was a disappointment for the marketing business unit. The business unit decided to drop this feature, which was not adding remarkable value.

- The marketing business unit also noticed that some customers were rating the dealer service quality performance very low, and this was negatively impacting other customers' buying decision. The team decided to fix this problem as follows: Customers would continue to rate dealer service quality via the mobile application, but the customer's rating would not be visible to other customers. It would only be visible to the CEC dealer management team.

5. Requirements Gathering

User requirements, functional requirements, nonfunctional requirements, and business rules of the product should be defined consistently with business requirements to keep the project on track and ensure the strategic, user, and technical fitness of the product.

- User requirements: what customer needs/goals the product should meet

- Functional requirements: what functionality the product should have in order to meet user requirements

- Nonfunctional requirements: how the product should work in terms of quality attributes, such as usability, performance, privacy, and security

- Business rules: mainly the conditions, constraints, and formulas that determine how requirements will be handled by the user and the product

If these user, functional and nonfunctional requirements, and business rules are not consistent with business requirements, then project outcomes will not deliver the desired value and fulfill customer needs. To mitigate this risk, business analysts should give highest priority to translating business needs into correct user requirements during requirements-gathering meetings. They should focus on resolving conflicts about these requirements before discussing the technical aspects of the product. They should always keep in mind that "doing the right thing is always more important than doing it right."

Business analysts should consider conflicts among project stakeholders positively during the requirements-gathering stage. If these conflicts are not discussed and resolved at this early stage of the project, they will later appear as high-cost CRs (change requests) at the development and testing phases. CRs are the main source of waste at PDLC because they

- can't be planned,

- result in scope creep,

- cause analysis paralysis,

- generate hidden costs,

- are mostly urgent,

- have both direct and indirect impacts on various parts of the product, and

- may bring a regression-testing burden.

In the lean approach, business analysts should be aware of factors that result in CRs and try to prevent them. The main reason for CRs is the "problems and deficiencies in requirements-gathering, documentation, and management process."

These kinds of CRs should be prevented in a proactive way by applying the following best practices throughout the requirements-gathering phase of a product development project:

- Realize that innovation cannot be achieved at the technical level. Innovation is a matter of formulating solutions that best meet user needs.

- During requirements-gathering meetings, be customer centric and ask, "What are customers' needs and how will the new product meet them?" instead of asking, "What should be the technical features of the new product?"

- Be open-minded, find alternative solution options, and prevent shallow "either/or" discussions about product features.

- Balance the level of creative vs. critical thinking at requirement-gathering meetings. At the beginning of the project, be as creative as possible. But when you start detailed requirement analysis, employ critical thinking. Critical thinking means asking the right, to-the-point questions and verifying them before assuming that they are correct.

- At the meetings, get ready to say no to even good ideas from the business units if these ideas are not in alignment with business and user requirements of the product.

- Although business analysts and project managers may have enough level of business and technical knowledge, technical teams should still be invited to requirements-gathering meetings to better evaluate the technical feasibility of requirements.

- Don't try to find the answers to why (we need the product), what (the product does), how (the product does), and technically how (the product works) questions during one single meeting. For large-scale projects, conduct separate sessions for interviews, focus groups, and workshops if your project is not a time-sensitive, fast-track one.

Go to the Gemba

- Don't listen to the voice of the customers only from product owners and business unit representatives. Elicitation techniques, such as shadowing, should be used to observe customers while using the products or their prototypes. In the lean approach, this is described as "go to the gemba."

Yes-Men vs. No-Men

- At requirements-gathering meetings, get ready to deal both with yes-men and no-men from business units. Yes-men are more dangerous than no-men. They are silent and friendly during requirements-gathering meetings but become aggressive and extremely demanding later at user acceptance tests. Although no-men are usually regarded as troublemakers, they are more helpful in identifying and resolving conflicts at the early stages of the project. Resolution of these early conflicts prevents waste due to costly change requests at later stages of the product development project.

Perfectionists vs. Overlookers

- In the lean approach, requirements gathered from both perfectionist and overlooking people should be analyzed carefully. Perfectionists usually focus on details of low-priority product features. On the other side, overlookers may mislead the project team by even undermining high-priority product features.

A Picture Is Worth a Thousand Words

- Benefit from prototyping during requirements-gathering meetings to help participants visualize the requirements in their minds.

Quantum Observer Effect

- The way of asking questions in requirements-gathering meetings is also important. The observer effect in quantum mechanics states that "by the act of watching, the observer affects the observed reality." Similarly, during requirements-gathering meetings, asking questions in a biased way impacts the objectivity of answers from participants.

- At requirements-gathering meetings, giving the right answers to wrong questions is more dangerous than giving wrong answers to the right questions. Wrong questions mislead the team, generate conflicts, waste project time, and result in failure. Business analysts should prepare simple, objective, and to-the-point questions for these meetings.

Conflict Is a Norm but Not an Exception

- At requirements-gathering meetings, don't be afraid of conflicts and negotiations among participants. The more conflicts resolved at this early stage means fewer CRs during the project.

- Try to clarify all of the issues during requirements-gathering meetings. Don't postpone them by entering into an issue database. Issue management means postponing problems.

- Don't feel desperate during requirements-gathering meetings when the number of conflicts increases and the problems get complicated. At those times, think that the project is not rocket science like at NASA or CERN, and do not exaggerate these situations. Instead of giving up early, remember the advice of Henry Ford: "There are no big problems; there are just a lot of little problems."

- Apply the "functional decomposition" technique to divide problems into smaller parts and resolve them one by one. When needed, benefit from the "five whys" technique, which is iteratively asking questions as a basis of the next question until finding the root cause of a particular problem.

Butterfly Effect in Chaos Theory

- When a change request is received, analyze its forward and backward impact on all levels of requirements. According to the Butterfly Effect in Chaos Theory, a small change at one place in a complex system can result in large effects elsewhere. The formation details of a hurricane can be influenced even by the flapping of a butterfly's wings at a distinct location several weeks earlier. This is also valid for CRs. A CR that is considered to be minor may result in a butterfly effect on lots of other product components and require a big effort.

6. Requirements Documentation

Features that customers do not use after the release are a big source of waste. The main reason for this problem is the lack of customer centricity during the traditional analysis and design approach.

Defining the details of user requirements by employing the "use case" technique in waterfall methodology and the "user story" technique in agile methodology helps project teams be more customer centric.

Use Case Technique:

In waterfall methodology's use case–driven analysis, user requirements are defined in three steps:

1. Who are the actors?

Target actors are defined.

2. What are the goals (use cases) of actors?

User requirements (use cases) correspond to the goals of the actors. Use cases are shown on a use-case diagram, which also illustrates the high-level scope.

For the CEC mobile application development project, the use case diagram below was defined:

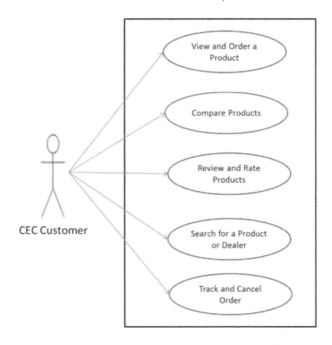

3. How will the actors achieve their goals?

In waterfall methodology, the activities of actors to achieve their goals can be shown on use case documents.

As mentioned earlier, the scope of the CEC mobile application project's first phase included only "View and Order a Product "and "Compare Products" use cases. The interaction of the CEC customers with the mobile application to achieve these goals was defined on use case documents. The "View and Order a Product" use case was documented as follows:

Use Case ID	01
Use Case Name	View and Order a Product
Actors	Customer
Description	Customer searches, finds, orders, and pays for an item.
Preconditions	Customer logs in to the system using an e-mail address and password.
Postconditions	Order confirmation report is sent to the user via e-mail. The dealer delivers the product.
Main Scenario	1. Customer navigates to product selection page. 2. Customer selects the product category (TV, DVD, speakers, etc.). 3. Customer views the displayed items under that category and selects a particular one. 4. Customer views details of the selected item (image, technical specs, color, size, availability, and price). 5. Customer adds the selected product to the shopping list. 6. Customer checks the accuracy of items on the shopping list. 7. Customer checks the total amount of the shopping list on the checkout page. 8. Customer enters shipping address. 9. Customer enters billing address. 10. Customer enters credit or debit card information. 11. Customer confirms the payment. 12. Customer views Order Confirmation Report. 13. Dealer gets the order (BR2). 14. Dealer delivers the product to the customer.
Alternative Scenario	1.1. Customer does a search for the product instead of navigating through the relevant category. 1.2. Customer views search results and selects the item he or she is looking for. 1.3. Back to step 4 of Main Scenario.

Exception Scenario	8.1. If customer selects fast delivery, he or she is notified with a message indicating that a commission rate will be charged for express deliveries (BR1).
	13.1. If the item is out of stock at every dealer, the customer is notified that "the selected product is currently out of stock" (BR2).
Nonfunctional Requirements	NFR 1. Performance: After the customer confirms the payment, the Order Confirmation Report should be displayed within two seconds.
	NFR 2. Usability: If the billing address is same as the delivery address, the customer does not have to enter the same data twice.
Business Rules	BR1. Express Delivery Commission = 1 percent
	BR2. The dealer nearest to the customer's shipping address delivers the ordered item. If the ordered item is out of stock at this dealer, the order is sent to the second-nearest dealer store.
Assumptions	A1. Product availability data received from the ERP inventory module is up to date and accurate.
	A2. Dealer location data received from dealer management system is up to date.

In use-case documentation, the following best practices should be considered:

- Scenarios on the use case document describe the activities of actors while achieving their goals.

- Each scenario step (activity) corresponds to a functional requirement.

While applying the use-case technique, there may be confusion about the difference between a use case and a functional requirement. Actually it is quite simple. Each use case represents a particular goal of an actor, whereas the activities to achieve that goal are functional requirements.

Let's explain this relationship with an analogy: If a bottle is considered a product, "drinking water" is a use case, since it is a goal of an actor in using the bottle. But "opening the bottle cap" is not a use case, because it is not a particular goal of the actor. People don't buy bottles to open and close their caps. Opening the bottle cap is just a functional requirement to reach the goal of "drinking water."

Similarly "View and Order a Product" is a use case for the CEC mobile application, whereas "category selection" is one of the several functional requirements to achieve that specific use case.

- Separate main, alternative, and exception scenarios of the use case.

The main scenario on a use case document represents the positive flow (happy path) of activities to achieve the goal of the actor in normal conditions.

Alternative scenarios define other possible ways of achieving the same goal.

Exception scenarios define the activities of the user in exceptional and error conditions.

For the "View and Order a Product" use case in the CEC mobile application, if finding an item by navigating through categories is described in the main scenario, then the discrete activities needed to find that item by using the "Search" functionality should be defined within an alternative scenario. The interaction between the customer and the CEC mobile application when the customer attempts to order an out-of-stock item should be defined as an exception scenario.

- Define exception scenarios separately from alternative scenarios.

Alternative scenarios may include some nice-to-have conditions that can be postponed until future releases, in case there is latency in the project. However, exception scenarios include error conditions, and they have to be implemented in any case.

- Use case documents aim to answer *what* (functionality needed in order to meet user requirements) and how (nonfunctional requirements and business rules) questions.

  Clarifying the *technically how* (inner technical dynamics) question is not a use case document's objective. Therefore, don't include technical details on use case documents. According to the "just in time" principle of the lean approach, technical requirements should be defined later in a separate technical design document.

- Define use case scenarios with the users' point of view, but don't include user interface details. Those details are defined later on prototypes and in user interface annotations based on use case scenario definitions.

  For example, "customer selects category by clicking buttons at the middle of the screen" is a wrong scenario activity definition. "Customer selects a category" is just enough.

- In addition to functional requirements, also define nonfunctional requirements, business rules, and assumptions on use case documents.

- Define business rules in a parametric way.

  This will let the project team easily design, develop, and change business rules when needed.

  For example, in the "View and Order a Product" use case, "User is notified with a message indicating that 1 percent commission will be charged for express deliveries" is a wrong functional requirement definition. Instead it should be defined as "User is notified with a message indicating that a commission rate will be charged for express deliveries (BR1)." Business rules in this scenario should be defined in the business rules section of the same use case document. The business rule in this example should be defined as follows:

  BR1: Express Delivery Commission = 1 percent

- Define nonfunctional requirements, such as usability, performance, and privacy, for each use case in a verifiable (testable) way.

  For example, "After the customer confirms the payment, an Order Confirmation Report should be displayed fast" is not a correct performance requirement definition. It should be defined as "After the customer confirms the payment, an Order Confirmation Report should be displayed within two seconds."

- Limit assumptions to the conditions in which the user has no control.

  For example, "Product availability data received from the ERP inventory module is up to date and accurate" may be an assumption for the "View and Order a Product" use case. But "the items that will be ordered by the customer are in stock" is not a correct assumption. The behavior of the customer and the CEC mobile application, in case the customer attempts to order an out-of-stock item, should be defined as an exception scenario on the use case document. Otherwise unclarified assumptions will create many issues at the user interface design, technical design, and development stages and result in waste due to unplanned work.

- Benefit from flow charts to visualize use case scenarios.

  In history, people first used drawings to communicate with one another. Even after the invention of letters, they continued to use drawings as an easy way of expressing themselves. Similarly, using diagrams such as flow charts is an effective way of visualizing use case scenarios and clarifying the ambiguities in narrative requirement definitions on plaintext, use case documents

  Flow charts are useful for modeling and describing work flows with simple diagramming conventions. A flow chart should be created for each use case. Each branch on a flow chart represents the main, alternative, or exception scenario of a use case.

  The flow chart below represents the "View and Order a Product" use case of the CEC mobile application. The branches on the chart show scenarios of that specific use case.

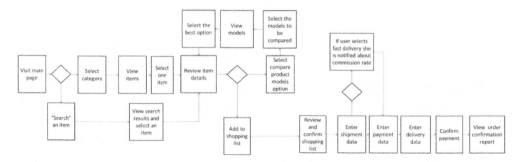

User Story Technique

Unlike waterfall, agile methodology focuses on "working products over comprehensive documentation."

In scrum, requirements are defined as short and simple user stories (As a "role," I want "goal") in parallel with the above manifesto statement.

As mentioned earlier, agile scrum methodology was applied at the second phase of the CEC mobile application project. Instead of detailed use case documents, simple user stories were defined at this phase.

Some of the user stories included in the product backlog of the CEC mobile application project were as follows:

- As a user, I can comment on CEC products so that other customers can learn about my experience.

- As a user, I can rate CEC products so that other users can benefit from my opinion in making their buying decisions.

- As a user, I can see the comments and ratings of customers posted via the mobile application, also on the CEC web page, so that I can make a better decision in product selection.

- As a user, I can search for the address of the nearest CEC dealer stores so that I can go and view the products I plan to buy.

- As a user, I can track the status of an order so that I can arrange my time for delivery of the product to my home.

- As a user, I can cancel my order on the mobile application so that I don't have to contact the call center.

- As a user, I can get campaign offers on the mobile application when I am near a dealer location so I can visit the store and view the product with a discounted price.

- As a user, I can get discount coupons when I connect to a CEC product via mobile application so that I can use them to pay less for my later purchases.

- As a user, I can log in to the CEC mobile application also with my social media accounts so that I can easily post information about CEC products.

User stories are lightweight compared to use cases. To make user stories more specific and descriptive for the development team, acceptance criteria should be defined for each user story. Acceptance criteria should also include nonfunctional requirements and business rules associated with each user story.

Some of the acceptance criteria defined for the CEC mobile application project were as follows:

User Story	Acceptance Criteria
As a user, I can comment on CEC products so that other customers can learn about my experience with CEC products.	- Only people who once purchased a CEC product on mobile application can post reviews. - A customer can make only one comment about a single product. - It is possible to comment on other customers' reviews. - Reviews cannot include advertisements or promotional material for other companies. - Reviews cannot include phone numbers or e-mail addresses. - Comments are limited to 200 characters.
As a user, I can get discount coupons when I connect to a CEC product via mobile application so that I can use them to pay less for my later purchases.	- When the customer activates Bluetooth on the mobile application, CEC products are listed. - The customer is able to select the CEC device he or she wants to connect to. - When connected, the customer receives a message that shows the

	discount coupon details.
	▪ The customer cannot earn additional discount coupons until he or she uses the existing ones.
As a user, I can search for the address of the nearest CEC dealer stores so that I can go and view the products I plan to buy.	▪ The customer can search for a dealer only through a product detail page. ▪ The mobile application lists the nearest dealer stores that have the specific product in stock. ▪ If the GPS of the customer's mobile phone is enabled, the application locates the customer's address automatically. ▪ The application displays the location of stores on a map.
As a user, I can track the status of an order so that I can arrange my time for delivery of the product to my home.	▪ The customer can view the real time status of his or her order. ▪ The order status types will be open, in progress, delivered, and cancelled.
As a user, I can cancel my order on the mobile application so that I don't have to contact the call center.	▪ The customer can query her orders. ▪ On the mobile application, the customer can only cancel the orders that have the status of "open" and "in progress." He or she can't cancel the orders that have the status of "delivered."
As a user, I can get campaign offers on the mobile application when I am near a dealer location so that I can visit the store and view the product with the discounted price.	▪ The campaign notification mode must be enabled in order to get offers. ▪ When the mobile application recognizes a customer located within the range of one mile or less

	to a CEC dealer store, the mobile application queries the CRM system for the most recent campaigns and notifies the customer.
	▪ The location mode (GPS) of the customer's mobile phone should be enabled.
	▪ If the customer does not want to get notification about campaigns, he or she can disable the notification mode.
As a user, I can log in to the CEC mobile application also with my social media accounts so that I can easily post information about CEC products.	▪ The customer can easily share the link of the product detail page by one click on a share button.

Do We Still Need Business Analysts in Agile Projects?

User stories are defined and prioritized on the product backlog by a business unit representative (product owner). He or she is the voice of the customer. In theoretical formulation there is no need for business analysts or their detailed requirements documents because the product owner and the agile development team, which consists of developers and QA (quality assurance) specialists, work together at the same location under the coordination of a scrum master.

However, in practice there are some difficulties in realizing this theoretical framework.

Product owners (lacking technical knowledge) have difficulties in speaking the same language with technical teams (with limited or no business knowledge). This makes it harder to translate business needs into requirements.

Additionally, product owners can rarely spend enough time with the agile team during their own department's busy times, and this makes the situation even more difficult.

To prevent these problems, business analysts have started to play the product owner role or have been involved in the technical team that used to be composed of only developers and QA specialists.

Whether it is waterfall or agile methodology, the following best practices should be applied in requirements documentation to prevent waste and ensure the best communication among project stakeholders:

Lean Principle of "Just Enough"

One of the main goals of the lean approach is eliminating waste by reducing work-in-process inventory (WIP). At PDLC unnecessarily long analysis and design documents represent WIP. To minimize WIP and eliminate waste, analysis and design documents should be "just enough." They should be concise without information overload. They should include only what is absolutely necessary.

As expressed in the phrase "A picture is worth a thousand words," business analysis diagrams, such as use case diagrams, flow charts, and context diagrams, should be used to decrease the information overload on requirements documents.

At the requirements documentation phase, the objective should not be to produce fancy documents and elegant diagrams that won't be read by any person other than the business analyst who prepared it. Instead, the objective should be to create products that best meet the business and customer needs by using requirements documents and diagrams as tools.

We need requirements documents during the project to translate business and customer needs into requirements for developers' best understanding, and after the project to use as a requirements repository during future enhancement/modification of products.

The detail level of documents should be calibrated according to specific project needs and conditions as to best satisfy the above objectives.

If the detail level of the documents is too low, there is a risk of incomplete requirements definition. In this case technical teams have to guess about product features. They build products that miss critical requirements, and this triggers a vicious cycle of CRs (change requests). And sometimes they build in extra features that are not included in the requirements documents, thinking that customers will be delighted to see them. This situation is called "gold plating." Both CRs and gold plating are factors that result in scope creep and thus waste during the project.

In daily life there would be chaos if there were no governing rules. For example, although traffic lights seem to slow us down, traffic would be locked without them. Requirement documents are like the traffic lights in big cities. If we don't use them, the project starts fast but is locked at some later stage. However, in small cities we don't need to locate traffic lights everywhere. Similarly, in small-scale projects we don't have to use very detailed requirements documents.

When team members are at discrete locations, this may limit the collaboration among project stakeholders. The same problem may be observed on outsourced projects. In these situations, the detail level of documents should be increased to ensure clarity and correctness of requirements.

The documents prepared during the analysis and design phase of the project also serve as a requirements repository. This makes the deployment of future product enhancements and modifications much easier and faster. Thus requirement documents should be kept updated even after the project to serve as a repository of requirements when needed during future modifications of the products. This will save a lot of time for the project team responsible for later enhancement/modification work and prevent a considerable amount of waste in the future.

Lean Principle of "Just in Time"

At PDLC,

- the answer of the "technically how" question (system requirements) depends on the answer of

- the "how" question (nonfunctional requirements and business rules), which depends on the answer of

- the "what" question (user requirements, functional requirements), which depends on the answer of

- the "why" question (business requirements).

According to the "Just in Time" principle in the lean approach, these questions should be answered in order and should be defined on separate documents.

First, the business requirements and user requirements should be defined and listed on business-case or vision and scope documents; then functional requirements, nonfunctional requirements, and business rules should be documented on use case documents or user stories, depending on the selected methodology. Then system requirements should be documented on technical design documents. Defining them in a single requirements document will create a lot of complexity and confusion for business units and technical teams.

7. UX Design and Usability

The best user experience (UX) on a product can be achieved only if usability is also positioned as a must-have requirement throughout the analysis and design process, in addition to functionality and visually aesthetic concerns.

Usability is the criterion that determines how easy a product is for its users. Even if it is very elegant and has great functionality, a product cannot fully meet the needs of its users unless it is usable. So unused features of the products create a huge amount of waste.

Gaudi Approach

Throughout the history of architecture design, Gaudi has been the most famous architect with his user-centered architecture design approach. During his childhood, Gaudi suffered from poor health. This situation prevented him from going to school, and he spent most of his time in nature. His observations of nature inspired his design approach, which can be summarized as follows: "The great book always open, and which we should make an effort to read, is that of Nature." Using this philosophy he designed buildings with "organic style," which then became an important standard in architecture.

Humanization of Products

Another man revolutionized the high-tech industry in a similar way. By positioning users at the center of the analysis and design process, Steve Jobs led the innovation of the most usable consumer electronics products ever.

He achieved creating natural-born users of his products. Even kids can use his company's mobile devices with gestures similar to their natural behavior. This new design approach made his company the best performer in the high-tech industry.

After the success of this approach, it was realized that the humanization of products is not necessarily achieved by anthropomorphic features but mainly by ensuring usability.

Building User Interfaces around Users

A lean UX design approach that is both user centered and iterative should be applied to ensure usability of a new product.

A. Identify User Profiles

"Designing for everybody" is not a feasible and effective strategy in terms of usability. Interfaces of a product are usable if they are a good fit for its users. Thus a product's user interface design should be based on the profile of its target user groups. Profiling can be done based on diverse user characteristics, such as:

- age,

- gender,

- education,

- computer use comfort level,

- smart phone comfort level, and

- business background.

For the CEC mobile application project, the profiling of customers was as follows:

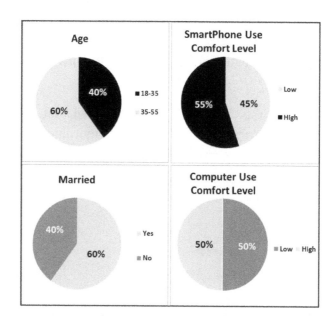

An effective way to understand user profiles during requirements-gathering sessions is to ask users their opinions about the existing products. Users' comments can be interpreted to understand their own capabilities and weaknesses. This reminds us of a quotation by the famous philosopher Spinoza: "If Pierre tells something about Paul, we learn more about Pierre than we learn about Paul."

In addition to interviews and focus group meetings with users, UX designers should also conduct field-analysis techniques—such as shadowing and user task analysis—to observe users in their own context and then profile them accordingly.

B. Define Personas and Their Mental Models

Another important aspect of user centricity is emotional design. Human beings judge products based on their left brains' logical and right brains' emotional capabilities. And most of the time, emotion is the main criterion in their judgments to buy a product.

In alignment with their emotions, users first create a mental model of the products they use. This model guides them throughout their whole experience with the product. Therefore, user interface designs should be based on the mental model of users rather than of designers.

Personas, which are representative imaginary characters, are the best way to define the mental models of diverse user profiles and predict their expected interaction with the product and behavior on user interfaces. Although there can be several user profiles for a product, UX designers should limit the number of personas to three (or at most four in extreme cases) to prevent falling into the trap of "designing for everybody." A persona description should include a name, a photo, demographic information, and a scenario section.

For the CEC mobile application project, the UX team defined the following two personas after analyzing user profiles and working with the marketing business unit.

Persona 1

"I have a very busy life"

John

Age: 24

Occupation: New Graduate

Marital Status: Single

Interests: Listening to music, playing video games

Technical Profile: Very comfortable with smartphone

I am a new graduate. Last month I started to work for a bank as a management trainee. I am working very hard during the week and mostly on Saturdays.

I love shopping, but I don't want to spend my only free time on Sunday doing that. I prefer to spend my time at home with friends and play video games. Due to my busy life, online shopping is a must-have rather than just a nice-to-have activity for me.

I love electronic devices, but currently I have a very limited budget. I usually don't miss any opportunity to get gift coupons and discount codes.

During the week I spend most of my time with my smartphone when I come home.

Persona 2

"Shopping is my hobby"

Melissa

Age: 35

Occupation: Housewife

Marital Status: Married

Interests: Watching TV shows and DVDs

Technical Profile: Beginner-level smartphone user

I have a newborn baby. My husband leaves home at 8:00 a.m. and returns at 8:00 p.m. from his office. Sometimes my friends visit me, but I usually spend the whole day at home alone with my baby.

When she sleeps I love watching TV shows and DVDs. Online shopping makes my life very easy since I cannot go out to shop. Additionally I like to comment on the products I buy and read reviews from other people.

But some of the online stores are difficult to use. I found a 3-D TV at a very good price on one of these sites, but, although I tried hard, I couldn't manage to purchase it with my discount code.

On my birthday my husband bought a smartphone for me. Yesterday I installed some social media applications, but I am not sure I will be able to use them.

C. Interaction Design

In the lean UX design approach, meeting user needs with a minimum number of steps on the product's user interfaces is highly appreciated. This can be achieved by a good interaction design.

"Architecture Begins Where Engineering Ends" —Walter Gropius

If well defined, flow charts visualizing use case scenarios form a perfect basis for design interaction of users with the product.

During interaction design, boxes on the branches of the flow chart are grouped within containers. These containers (dashed boxes) become a primary user-interface window, a dialogue box, or a message box. Or several containers combine and form a single user interface. Links between flow chart containers become navigation elements, such as links. This method, which is mainly based on the grouping of requirements, mitigates the risk of missing any functionality on user interfaces of the product. It also prevents mismatch between the flow of use case scenarios and the flow of user interfaces, and ensures usability.

For the CEC mobile application project, flow charts were used for interaction design as follows:

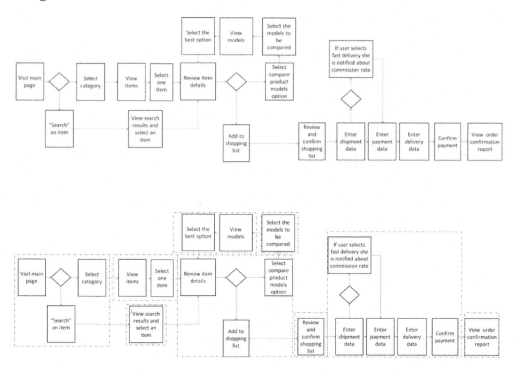

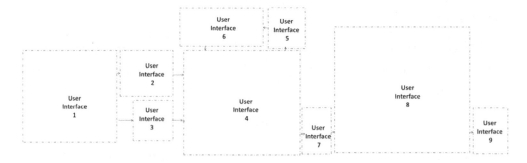

D. Information Architecture

User interfaces of products are composed not only of functional requirements (tasks) but also of content requirements.

Therefore, in parallel to interaction design (based on functional requirements), the information architecture (based on content requirements) should also be designed. The main objective of information architecture design is to identify content requirements, define content categories, and finalize the navigation structures of a product's user interfaces by using techniques such as card sorting and wireframes.

In the lean approach, the content on the user interfaces of a product should have two main attributes:

- **Concise:**

    o   Have statements that are short and to the point

    o   Leave no room for misinterpretation

    o   Have content that is simple and expressed with a minimum number of words.

    This quotation from Mark Twain describes this situation very well: "I didn't have time to write a short letter, so I wrote a long one instead."

- **Useful:**

    o   The content on user interfaces should remove the friction of product with its users. User interfaces should speak the language of users, not the technical teams.

- o Rather than offering a one-size-fits-all approach, the content should address the   information needs of target personas. Persona representatives should feel that the   content   on   the product's user interfaces is created especially for them.

- o Content should have clear links and CTAs (call to actions) that help users navigate intuitively without too much thinking.

Card-Sorting

If content is not grouped correctly, users will have difficulty finding what they are looking for on the product's user interfaces. This is a common type of usability defect.

Card-sorting is an effective information architecture technique to prevent this risk. It is used to categorize content.

In the card-sorting technique, content items are written on cards, and users who represent personas are asked to group these items.

By using a card-sorting study, the CEC mobile application's product category structure was defined as follows:

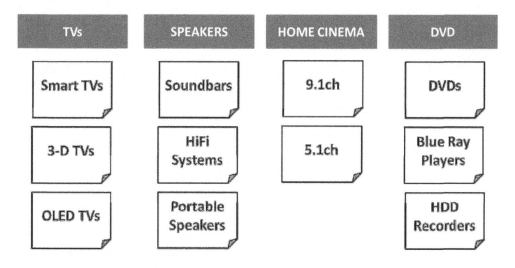

E. User Interface Design

UX designers convert interaction designs and information architectures into user interfaces of products by applying UX design and usability principles.

Even the most experienced designers can't produce the optimum design at the first trial. Good design is a result of several iterations. Iteration is a cycle of doing something, testing it, improving it, and retesting it.

Making iterations on the final product is a very costly approach. Because for every iteration, the technical components of the product have to be changed and retested, whereas changing the prototype is much easier and faster compared to changing the final product.

In the lean approach, the project team and customers should frequently come together and evaluate the functionality and usability of the product early on prototypes.

Recent prototyping tools allow mocking up the products and simulating them in an interactive way. They allow user actions, such as navigating between interfaces, selecting options, and getting notifications by error messages. Thanks to these interactive features, both functionality- and usability-related defects can be found and fixed at the early stages of the project without waiting for user acceptance tests on the final product.

By this iterative approach, a high number of CRs can be prevented. Also early detection of defects, without waiting for late user-acceptance tests, reduces the cost of fixing them and eliminates waste.

In the lean approach, prototypes are also considered work-in-process inventory. Thus, instead of mocking up every user interface and creating waste, UX designers should create the prototypes of user interfaces corresponding only to the most frequently used, high-priority features.

For the CEC mobile application project, the BA-Works team only mocked up user interfaces of the high-priority product features that were developed with the waterfall approach at the first phase of the project. To achieve simplicity, the mobile application's user interfaces included everything users needed and nothing they didn't.

Having interaction designs based on well-prepared use cases and flow charts made it easy for the project team to create prototypes of high-priority features that made up the core version of the product. The team detected and fixed functionality- and usability-related defects early on the prototype before releasing it in the market. This prevented a considerable amount of waste due to potential CRs.

Do We Need Prototypes in Agile Projects?

As mentioned earlier, agile methodology was applied at the second phase of the CEC mobile application project. To minimize WIP inventory, our team didn't prototype user stories. Instead working parts of the mobile application corresponding to user stories were used for functional and usability testing.

For agile projects, if user stories have the right level of granularity and are atomic, working parts of the product can be developed quickly and used for functional and usability testing instead of spending extra time for prototyping.

Picasso-Perfect Designs

During prototyping, UX designers and business analysts may hesitate when considering whether to behave like a craftsman or an artist. Until the Renaissance, the majority of architects designed their artifacts with a craftsman approach. Aesthetics were still important for architects, but their main concern was designing buildings, bridges, and fountains that best met the needs of the public. After the freedom and creativity impact of the Renaissance, architects started to behave more like artists and focused on designing more aesthetic pieces.

Instead of trying to create Picasso-perfect designs with an artistic approach, business analysts and UX designers should always behave like craftsmen during prototyping. They should focus on meeting the functional needs of customers in the most usable way, leaving aesthetic concerns to visual designers. In summary they should create prototypes that mainly show how the product's user interfaces will interact with users without its visual bells and whistles.

Less is *Much* More in the Lean Approach

With the lean approach, user interfaces of products should be designed simple enough to leave no need for learning how to use the product. The best user interfaces are simplistic and intuitive ones, on which users can easily find what they are looking for and complete their tasks with minimum effort and error.

On the opposite side, busy and noisy interfaces make the experience complicated for users. This kind of design can be easily created by distributing the functional specs randomly on different parts of user interfaces without too much design thinking.

Legendary soccer player Johan Cruyff once said, "Football is simple. But nothing is more difficult than playing simple football." Similarly, it is not that easy to create simplistic and intuitive user interface designs. Simplistic designs require extra time and effort.

The secret to achieving simplicity in design is best explained in the quotation from famous novelist Antoine de Saint Exupery: "A designer knows he has achieved perfection not when there is nothing left to add, but when there is nothing left to take away."

However, in simplifying user interfaces, an Einstein quotation should also be remembered to prevent the risk of false simplicity: "Everything should be made as simple as possible, but not simpler." The unnecessary parts of the user interface should be removed to make the interfaces simpler, unless removing these parts clears away any product functionality.

Customer Journey Mapping

For the CEC mobile application project, our team applied a customer experience evaluation technique called *customer journey mapping* in addition to traditional usability testing methods.

Customer journey mapping was an effective tool to visualize and evaluate the end-to-end experience of CEC customers at different touch points. From the customers' own perspective, their experience, emotions, and satisfaction level at each part of the journey were visualized.

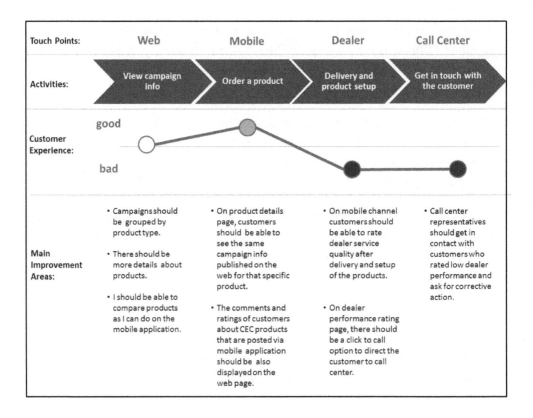

Touch Points:	Web	Mobile	Dealer	Call Center
Activities:	View campaign info	Order a product	Delivery and product setup	Get in touch with the customer
Customer Experience:	good ⟶ bad			
Main Improvement Areas:	• Campaigns should be grouped by product type. • There should be more details about products. • I should be able to compare products as I can do on the mobile application.	• On product details page, customers should be able to see the same campaign info published on the web for that specific product. • The comments and ratings of customers about CEC products that are posted via mobile application should be also displayed on the web page.	• On mobile channel customers should be able to rate dealer service quality after delivery and setup of the products. • On dealer performance rating page, there should be a click to call option to direct the customer to call center.	• Call center representatives should get in contact with customers who rated low dealer performance and ask for corrective action.

In addition to exploring improvement areas for interaction channels, this study also helped the team determine whether desired value was created for customers at each touch point.

For instance, at the second phase of the project, the following additional features were identified as an outcome of the customer journey mapping study:

- Customers should be able to rate and comment on dealer service quality after delivery and setup of the products.

- Comments and ratings of customers about CEC products that are posted via the mobile application should be also displayed on the web page.

8. Technical Design

Refactoring and Tolerance for Future Changes

Due to the iterative nature of the lean approach, the technical architecture of a product should allow revisions with new and updated features at later releases.

During iterative development, if the product has intensive integration among its components the following happens:

The team delivers product parts A and B without any major problems at initial iterations. Nevertheless, the team realizes that it has to make changes to parts A and B while working on part C since it has integration points with those parts. In other words, A and B have to be refactored although they have already been released.

Refactoring means changing the existing technical architecture of a product without changing its behavior, and it is always harder than developing from scratch. These back-and-forth moves with challenging refactoring efforts make the build and delivery of the product with integrated components even more difficult at later iterations.

Spaghetti Architectures

These frequent refactoring efforts necessitate excellent architecture design and development skills within the technical team. Whether the selected methodology is agile or waterfall, architects should formulate a highly flexible technical architecture design. Otherwise the architecture will be more like spaghetti with additions and updates at following iterations. This will result in a fragile product with performance, security, predictability, and reliability problems.

Flexible Data Models

To build a highly flexible technical architecture, the data model of the product should be parametric and flexible. This way excessive data migration and conversion needs, due to new transactional and reporting requirements, can be prevented.

During the requirements-gathering phase of the CEC mobile application project, the BA-Works team defined the reporting requirements. They included:

- Share of mobile channel in total sales revenue

- Mobile channel sales revenue by dealer

- Mobile channel sales revenue by product category

- Mobile channel sales revenue by product

- Conversion rate showing how many customers ordered a product when they used the mobile application

- Effectiveness of contextual campaign notifications displayed on the mobile application.

To create a flexible technical architecture, BA-Works business analysts considered all transactional and reporting needs for the CEC mobile application when designing its data model, which is shown below.

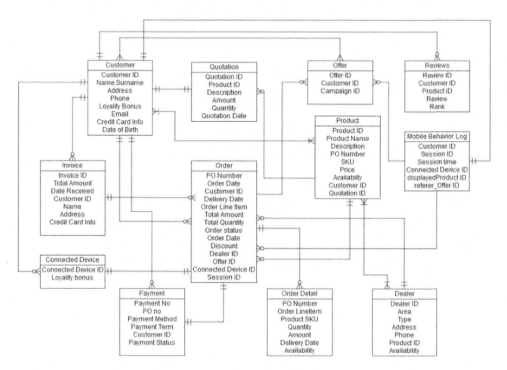

Performance and Reliability

In the lean approach, the elegance of a product is not only limited to its visual aspects. An elegant product is one that proposes maximum value for its customers with the highest level of reliability and performance. The major factor that makes a product fragile is its technical complexity. This is usually a result of embedding an excessive number of features into a product that has limited hardware capacity.

One of the solutions for this problem is to build an open technical architecture that allows the product to communicate with other products by transmitting data between them and sharing their complementary features. This way, a single product does not have to include all those features within it. This kind of open technical architecture is the main driver behind wearable technologies' capabilities that are beyond their own capacity.

For instance, users of a simple, wearable step counter can also manage their diet and personal training programs via its mobile interfaces by connecting to other products such as electronic scales and fitness devices.

Big Data

In time the data generated by products may reach to a big scale. This level of data can't be stored within them due to limited hardware capacity. To overcome this challenge, the data can be stored and managed on the cloud. However, this will only create data-level waste unless companies utilize big data technologies to generate valuable insights for users of their products.

For instance, the wearable step counters mentioned earlier provide helpful and motivating insights, such as comparing the user's activity and diet statistics with other users' results. They also do real-time analysis of the user's daily activity and diet data and send notifications in case they can't fulfill the target levels. Such big data insights enrich the value proposition of these products from being simple step counters to healthy life assistants.

DevOps

Due to the iterative nature of the lean approach, the product goes live in multiple releases. Sometimes the products developed within planned time frames cannot be released on time because of deployment problems.

To mitigate deployment risks, such as latencies, high failure rates, and long fixing and recovery times, operations teams should start working together with technical teams during the design and development of the products and always be synchronized with them. Otherwise deployment will always be a bottleneck and create *operational-level waste* at every release of the product.

9. Quality Assurance and Testing

In the lean approach, product defects result in quality-level waste due to the time and resources spent to find, fix, and retest them.

To eliminate this kind of waste, principles of global QA and testing organizations, such as ISTQB® (International Software Testing Qualifications Board), should be applied within the product development life cycle:

Testing shows presence of defects.

Testing shows the presence of defects but cannot prove zero defects. Testing efforts reduce the number of undiscovered defects on the product but cannot claim zero defects.

In the lean approach, the balance between time to market and product quality should be well established. Although not desired, a product may even go live with low-priority defects in case time to market is highly critical. This usually happens at the first iteration of a project in order to release a product earlier than competitors. These defects can then be fixed at later iterations.

Exhaustive testing is impossible.

Testing every single part of a product is not possible due to time and resource limitations. In the lean approach, testing efforts should focus on high-risk areas instead of exhaustive testing. Risk prioritization should be done according to potential impact and likelihood levels. This way, the waste due to excessive testing efforts can be prevented.

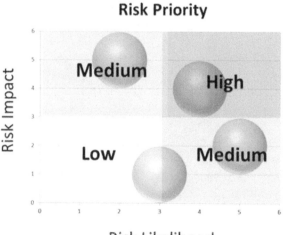

For most of the projects, requirement documents are used as a basis for test cases. However, test cases should not only contain positive scenarios on requirement documents; they should also cover negative test conditions. These negative test conditions can be identified by applying risk-based testing techniques, such as FMEA (Failure Mode and Effect Analysis).

Applying black-box test techniques, such as equivalence partitioning, boundary value, and combinatorial analysis, helps to achieve enough test coverage with minimum test data. These techniques prevent waste by eliminating the need for excessive test data.

Early testing

The product development life cycle is like a river with requirements at its source. If you can't clean the river at its source, you will have a dirty river flowing down the hill. A reactive rather than a proactive approach to clean the river will increase the costs and risks exponentially.

Due to the gravity of this situation, quality assurance teams should be more proactive and start testing as early as possible during the product development life cycle. Resolution of early defects prevents waste due to costly fixes at later stages. Without waiting for the development of the final product, testing should be started early by reviews on requirement documents and user tests on prototypes. By doing this both functionality- and usability-related defects can be easily found and fixed at the early phases of the project.

Pesticide paradox

If the same kinds of tests are repeated again and again, the same set of test cases will no longer help to find any new defects on the product. To overcome this "pesticide paradox," the test cases should be regularly reviewed and updated. Thus the waste due to ineffective testing efforts will be prevented.

To ensure enough coverage, QA teams should form the test basis according to requirements and business rules on analysis documents and combine them with risk-based test conditions.

During phase one of the CEC mobile application project, the "View and Order a Product" test case was defined as follows based on main, alternative, and exception scenarios of the relevant use case document:

Test Case ID	01	
Test Case Name	View and Order a Product	
Actors	Customer	
Description	Customer searches, finds, orders, and pays for an item.	
Preconditions	Customer logs in to the system using e-mail address and password.	
Postconditions	Order confirmation report is sent to the user via e-mail. The dealer delivers the product.	
Steps	**Main Scenario**	**Expected Results**
1	Customer navigates to product selection page.	System displays all product categories.
2	Customer selects the product category (TV, DVD, Speaker, etc.).	All of the relevant products under that category are displayed.
3	Customer views the displayed items under that category and selects a particular one.	System displays valid products.
4	Customer views details of the selected item (image, technical specs, color, size, availability, and price).	System selects and displays valid product details from content management and ERP systems.
5	Customer adds the selected product to the shopping list.	System creates valid data on the quotation table.
6	Customer checks the accuracy of items on the shopping list.	System displays accurate shopping list data.
7	Customer controls the total amount of the shopping list on the check-out page.	System displays valid total amount.
8	Customer enters shipping address.	System checks the validity of data according to data entry rules.
9	Customer enters billing address.	System checks the validity of data according to data entry rules.
10	Customer enters credit or debit card information.	System asks for confirmation.
11	Customer confirms the payment.	System communicates with payment channel and gets payment confirmation.
12	Customer views the 'Order Confirmation Report'.	System creates accurate order data on order table.
13	Dealer gets the order.	Ordered item is directed to the dealer nearest to the customer.

		If the ordered item is out of stock at this dealer, the order is sent to the second-nearest dealer store.
14	Dealer delivers the product to the customer.	Order status is updated as delivered.
Steps	**Alternative Scenario**	**Expected Results**
15	1.1. Customer searches the product instead of navigating through the relevant category.	System displays valid search results
16	1.2. Customer views search results and selects the item he or she is looking for.	System selects and displays valid product details from content management and ERP systems.
17	1.3. Back to step 4 of Main Scenario.	System displays valid selection data.
Steps	**Exception Scenario**	**Expected Results**
18	8.1 Customer selects fast delivery.	Customer is notified with a message indicating that a commission rate will be charged for express deliveries. The commission rate is calculated correctly.
19	13.1 Customer orders an out-of-stock item.	Customer is notified as "the selected product is currently out of stock".

As shown on the above example, use case documents that have detailed scenarios form a good basis for test cases. When agile methodology is applied, however, user stories and their acceptance criteria do not have that level of detail. To ensure enough test coverage, QA teams on agile projects should work in high collaboration with product owners and other business unit representatives during the tests.

Automated Testing

In lean's iterative approach, adding new components to a live product without impacting its already released parts is like changing the tire of a car while it's moving.

This iterative development approach requires comprehensive regression testing of the product components that were already released in previous iterations. To ensure enough test coverage, the parts with both direct and indirect integration points should be retested. This brings a huge amount of extra testing effort. Testing the same components manually and repetitively is both time-consuming and impractical. To make this process more efficient, automated regression test suites can be created.

However, automation itself is a challenging project. Project managers should consider the time needed to implement automation tools as a separate risk item in every project. They should not use an automation tool for the first time in a time-sensitive, high-priority project. The team should focus on the project, instead of allocating its limited time for tool implementation. Project managers should remember that upper management always takes account of the score but not how the team played during the game.

In an automated regression-testing process, test procedures are captured as test scripts at the first test cycle and then run automatically in following test cycles. However, test automation is not a magic way of finding defects by pressing a single button. Most of the time technical problems arise on test automation tools during test script generation. Fixing these problems requires advanced technical skills. For this reason test automation should always be the responsibility of technical QA teams rather than business analysts.

In some circumstances manual testing becomes more efficient than automated testing; it takes much more time to generate automated test scripts compared to running test cases manually. Especially in time-sensitive, fast-track projects, this results in a weird situation of coding around bugs instead of finding and fixing them. Project managers and QA managers should consider this issue as a project risk. They should mitigate this risk by determining the right level of test automation.

Shelfware

In recent years, we have started to see a different "ware" category (like hardware and software). This category is called *shelfware*. Shelfware represents the automation software that sits on the shelves of the company without being used by any single person.

Shelfware causes a huge amount of *tool-level waste*. At some public companies, high license and support costs paid for useless shelfware has even become an issue investigated during internal audits.

To prevent shelfware situation, managers should know that automation tools are wizards but not magicians. They have limits. They can only help the project team do its work in a more convenient way by automating some of the tasks, but not all of them. If the organization's QA process maturity is at a good level, automation makes it better; otherwise, automation may even make it worse. Hence managers should first focus on improving their QA and testing skills and then give the go-ahead for the automation initiative. If the team has only limited knowledge of test methods and techniques, automation will only bring extra problems rather than benefits.

UAT Is the Last Filtering Point of Defects.

Even with the existence of a separate QA team, business analysts should be in charge of coordinating and guiding business units during UAT (user acceptance tests). UAT is the final stage for validating requirements and ensuring the fulfillment of business needs of the new product. In case UAT is not conducted effectively, end users will find defects after the release, and this will result in money and reputation loss.

To increase the effectiveness of UAT, users should first conduct experience-based tests without running any test cases. Afterward another UAT cycle should be organized to ensure enough test coverage by running UAT cases. Business analysts can prepare UAT cases by simplifying the test cases generated by QA teams.

Normally user training should be provided after UAT if the new product is replacing an existing one. Users will be able to test the product in a more independent and unbiased way. But, if the product is a new one, user training should be conducted before UAT. Otherwise users will have difficulties in using the product, which is completely new to them, and this will result in lower test coverage ratios and longer UAT durations.

10. Project Management

While project managers are responsible for *project scope* management, business analysts are responsible for *product scope* management.

Product scope represents the features of the product to meet business and user requirements, whereas project scope is defined as the work that needs to be accomplished to build and release the product with these specified features. Therefore, in order to define the project scope correctly, the project manager should assist business analysts in defining a clear and correct product scope aligned with business and user requirements. Otherwise resources are rooted in the wrong direction, and this results in *project-level waste*.

Output Trap

In addition to scope management, time and cost management are the other critical knowledge areas in project management. Sometimes the pressure to meet time and budget targets can lead project managers to focus more on generating outputs (deliverables) than on outcomes (value). However, if the requirements cannot be met, the project won't be successful even if it is completed on time and within budget constraints. To prevent this "output" trap and assure the delivery of value-adding "outcomes," project managers should always work in collaboration with business analysts to ensure value creation at every step of the project. They should keep all project stakeholders connected throughout the product development lifecycle.

To achieve this, project managers should manage the project in the field. Some project managers spend most of their time at the PMO (project management office) instead of attending requirements-gathering meetings, reviewing requirements documents, and participating in testing sessions.

In the lean approach, project managers should go to the gemba and have high bandwidth communication with project stakeholders and customers throughout the product development lifecycle.

Whole Optimization Instead of Suboptimization

The lean approach aims to remove the checks and balances within project stakeholders to ensure collaboration.

Although segregation of duties is important to manage accountability among team members, it should not result in silos.

Silos usually form due to micromanagement of separate teams such as business analysts, designers, developers, and quality assurance specialists. Micromanagement results in the suboptimization of each group's objectives with output-oriented KPIs (key performance indicators), such as the number of requirements documented, number of defects found, or number of codes built. But in the lean approach, KPIs aim to optimize the objectives of the whole team. For instance, KPIs such as "the number of user requirements satisfied at a specific release" or "percent of business requirement targets met at first release" will help the project manager keep every project stakeholder motivated in the same direction to generate desired value for customers.

In applying the lean approach for the first time, project managers should remember that "it is not the strength of waves that shapes the rocks, but it is their persistence." Thus, instead of giving up early, they should continuously motivate their teams to apply lean principles and techniques to their projects by managing any kind of internal resistance.

End of the Story at the CEC Company

Thanks to applying the lean approach to the CEC mobile application development project, the project team managed to be value oriented, customer centered, and iterative throughout the project. This helped the CEC company satisfy all of the below project objectives:

- Differentiate itself by having a mobile channel earlier than all other consumer electronics companies

- Be innovative in creating a mobile sales channel with features that were directly driven by CEC customer needs

- Prevent waste by only investing in features that were really necessary

- Improve scale that was once limited to the number and visibility of dealers

- Satisfy the marketing business unit by releasing the mobile application at the time they requested

- Be aware of risks early and mitigate them quickly

The project was completed on time to the high satisfaction of all project stakeholders. For this project, upper management realized the benefits of the lean approach and decided to apply this approach to all other projects.

Index

Made in United States
North Haven, CT
12 December 2021

12614462R00050